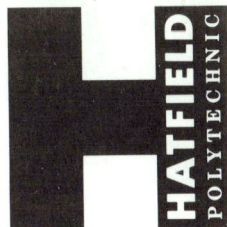

Design   David West Children's Book Design
Illustrations   George Thompson
Picture Research Cee Weston-Baker

The publishers wish to thank Nigel Norris B.V.Sc. M.R.C.V.S. for his assistance in the preparation of this book.

First published in Great Britain in 1989 by
Franklin Watts Ltd, 96 Leonard Street, London EC2A 4RH

© Aladdin Books Ltd 1989

Designed and produced by
Aladdin Books Ltd, 70 Old Compton Street, London W1V 5PA

ISBN 0 7496 0084 5

A CIP catalogue record of this book is available from the British Library.

Printed in Belgium

Contents

BABY ANIMALS

Puppies

Kate Petty

Franklin Watts
London · New York · Toronto · Sydney

Newborn puppies

A mother dog – or bitch – is pregnant for about nine weeks. She needs a quiet place to have her puppies and it is best to leave her alone when she is ready to give birth. Within hours she might have as many as 12 tiny puppies. She will lick each puppy clean as soon as it is born.

The mother Spaniel gives the new puppy its first wash.

This bitch's puppies are due any day now. ▷

Early days

Each newly-washed puppy instinctively finds its way to one of its mother's nipples and starts to drink her milk. The little puppies soon grow fat and round. Feeding them all is hard work for the mother and she needs extra food for herself. She might be cross if people come too close to her puppies.

Two-day-old Labrador puppies drinking milk from their mother

A basketful of 30-day-old Golden Retriever puppies ▷

First impressions

Newborn puppies can neither see nor hear their new world. It is their keen sense of smell that guides them to their mother's milk. The puppies start to hear after about three days. Soon they will prick up their ears at the slightest sound. Their eyes are not fully open until they are about two weeks old.

Young Alsatian

Five-week-old Border Collie sniffing the ground ▷

Learning to walk

While they are still babies the puppies spend most of their time feeding or sleeping. After about three weeks the more adventurous ones start to use their legs and the others soon follow. At first they stagger about unsteadily but before long they are running, jumping and playing.

This Jack Russell puppy is ready to run about.

Soon this Sheepdog puppy will be off to explore. ▷

Playing

Playful puppies are fun to watch. They are learning all sorts of things about each other as they play. Wild dogs live in packs that hunt together. They need to know which one is boss. A litter of puppies is like a little pack. They decide which one is the strongest by play-fighting. When a puppy lies on its back it admits that it is weaker than its opponent.

Greyhound puppies playing together

Which Border Collie pup will be the first to surrender? ▷

Mischief

Little puppies often get into mischief, although it is not always their fault. Sometimes they can't wait any longer to go outside, and make puddles on the floor. When they are teething, at around four months, they need to be given things that they are allowed to chew. Otherwise a puppy can chew all the wrong things...

Puppies make many mistakes. This is a Wire-haired Dachshund.

This Bernese Mountain dog has found a stick to chew. ▷

Resting

Even though they need plenty of sleep when they are small, most puppies and young dogs would rather be running around and playing than lying down. All that exercise makes a puppy pant. When it pants and hangs out its tongue a dog is cooling off. Soon it will be on the go again. Puppies like a basket or a rug of their own to sleep on at night.

This mongrel puppy stops for a breather.

This three-and-a-half-week-old puppy fell asleep on his way back to the basket. ▷

Eating

Puppies grow very quickly. They stop drinking their mother's milk at about five weeks old. Then they need twice as much food as an adult dog for a while. Puppies should have four little meals a day until they are three months old, gradually reduced to one or two meals by the time they are nine months. Beef bones are best for gnawing on. Chicken bones can splinter and be harmful.

Scottish Terrier puppy enjoying a bone

Puppies must have water to drink. ▷

Communicating

The whole of a puppy's little body is as expressive as its face. You can tell whether it is happy or sad simply from its tail! Dogs bark and howl to call the other members of the pack – or of the family, if they are pet dogs. Be careful with a growling puppy – it is warning you to stay away.

This Dalmatian puppy wags its tail to show it is pleased.

What is this little Scottish Terrier trying to say? ▷

Lessons to learn

More than any other baby animal, a puppy has to be trained as soon as it is old enough to understand. Wild dogs learn to obey the leader of the pack. In the same way, pet dogs are willing to obey a sensible owner. Nobody likes a disobedient dog. A dog that chases sheep or runs out into traffic is a real danger.

A puppy must learn to wait at the kerb.

Border Collie pups learning to fetch ▷

Puppy facts

Some small dogs are fully grown at six months. Some big dogs are still puppies at a year old. Poodles like these reach their full size at about nine months. They can be expected to live for eight or nine years. The smaller breeds of dog generally live several years longer than the larger ones.

Newborn

Adult male

Adult female

Index

Photographic credits:
Cover and pages 3, 5, 7, 9, 11, 15 and 21: Jane Burton/Bruce Coleman Ltd; page 13: Hans Reinhard/Bruce Coleman Ltd; page 17: J. Allan Cash Picture Library; page 19: Frank Lane Picture Agency.